Big Machines for Fun and Sport

Geoff Thompson

Contents

All kinds of big machines	4
Motorbikes	6
Motor racing	8
Campervans	10
Fun boats	12
Motor boats	13
Sailing boats	14
Houseboats	16
Hot-air balloons	18
Gliders	20
Hang-gliders	22
Questions	24
Glossary	24
Index	25

All kinds of big machines

People use all kinds of big machines
for having fun,
for playing sport,
and for going on holidays.

Machines like these are very exciting.

motorbike

racing cars

sailing boat

hot-air balloons

campervan

hang-glider

Motorbikes

Many people love motorbikes because they are fun to ride.

Motorbikes are much smaller than other vehicles, and can move quickly. They are easy to ride in the city.

Motorbikes are good for riding out on the open road.

Some people ride their motorbikes in races, too.

Motor racing

Many people love to watch motor races. Fast cars speed around a race track.

DID YOU KNOW?

Cars that go in motor races have special wheels and wide tyres.

Some motor races are held on special race tracks.
Other races are held on city roads.
These roads are closed to other cars while the race is on.

Campervans

Some people use campervans when they go on holidays.

A campervan is like a small house on wheels.

People can sit and sleep in a campervan. They can cook and eat there, too.

DID YOU KNOW?

Some campervans have showers in them.

Fun boats

There are all kinds of boats that people use for having fun and for going on holidays.

There are motor boats, sailing boats, and houseboats.

motor boat

sailing boat

houseboats

Motor boats

People use motor boats for fishing, for water-skiing or just for moving around on the water.

Big motor boats often have cabins to sleep in.

Sailing boats

Sailing boats have big sails that puff out in the wind.

Some sailing boats have small motors, too.

Sailing boats can be used for racing or for fun.

Houseboats

Sometimes people like to stay
on houseboats for their holidays.
Houseboats have rooms
for people to sleep in.

Houseboats can float on rivers,
or on water
where the waves are not too big.

People can sit on the deck of a houseboat. They can fish and go swimming from the deck, too.

Hot-air balloons

People go for rides in hot-air balloons.
They stand in a big basket
that hangs under the balloon.

Hot-air balloons move slowly.

Lift-off and landing

1. A gas burner blows hot air into the balloon.

2. The hot-air balloon floats up high.

3. When the pilot turns off the gas, the balloon comes down again.

Gliders

A glider is like a small plane without an engine.

It has long, thin wings.

DID YOU KNOW?

Some gliders can fly for 1000 km before coming down to land.

Gliders are pulled along on a rope
by a plane or a car.
When the glider is high enough in the air,
the pilot of the plane,
or the driver of the car, lets the rope go.
Then the glider can fly by itself.

The wind under the wings
helps to keep the glider
from falling to the ground.

Hang-gliders

A hang-glider is a bit like an enormous kite. Hang-gliders take off from cliffs or hilltops.

The pilot holds onto a bar
under the wings of the hang-glider,
as it swoops and glides through the air.

The hang-glider comes down to the ground
very slowly.

Questions

1. What are the tyres and wheels like on cars that go in motor races?

2. What do some campervans have in them?

3. How far can some gliders fly before landing?

Glossary

cabin	a place to sleep on a boat
deck	wooden floor of a ship or boat
gas burner	a machine that makes hot air
sail	part of a boat or a ship that helps to move it through the water